VOL. 19

HAL•LEONARD®
KEYBOARD
PLAY-ALONG™

Jazz Classics

Featuring the Jazz Arts Trio

T0085041

The Jazz Arts Trio is:
Frederick Moyer - Piano
Peter Tillotson - Bass
Peter Fraenkel - Drums

www.jrirecordings.com

All transcriptions by Frederick Moyer
except "Watch What Happens" by Forrest "Woody" Mankowski

ISBN 978-1-4234-8502-5

HAL•LEONARD®
CORPORATION
7777 W. BLUEMOUND RD. P.O. BOX 13819 MILWAUKEE, WI 53213

Visit Hal Leonard Online at
www.halleonard.com

DISCOGRAPHY

Blues Etude

as played by Oscar Peterson - from the DVD *The Berlin Concert*

(They Long to Be) Close to You

as played by Erroll Garner - from the album *Magician*

Freeway

as played by Vince Guaraldi - from the album *In Person*

Lonely Woman

as played by Horace Silver - from the album *Song for My Father*

My Foolish Heart

as played by Bill Evans - from the album *Live at the Village Vanguard*

Tin Tin Deo

as played by Oscar Peterson – from the album *Easy Walker!*

Watch What Happens

as played by Oscar Peterson - from the album *Tristeza on Piano*

Blues Etude

By Oscar Peterson

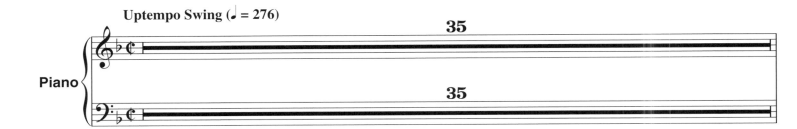

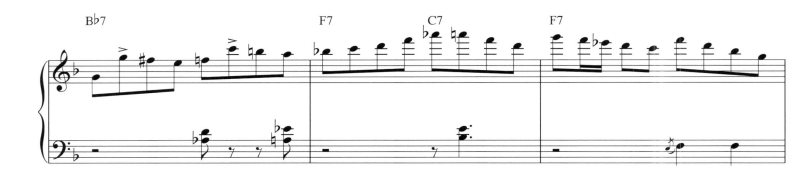

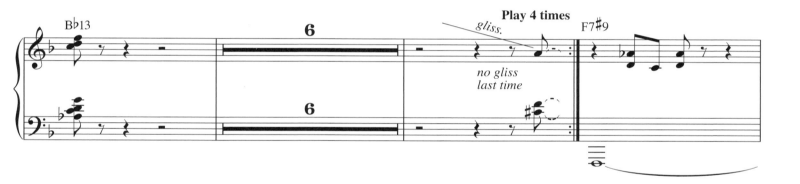

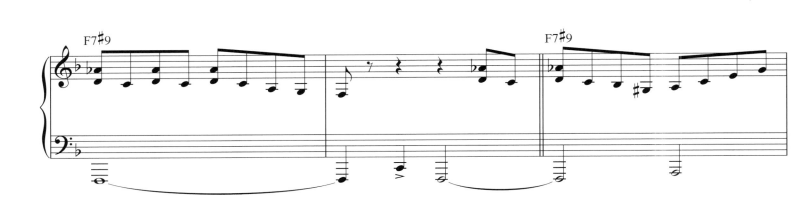

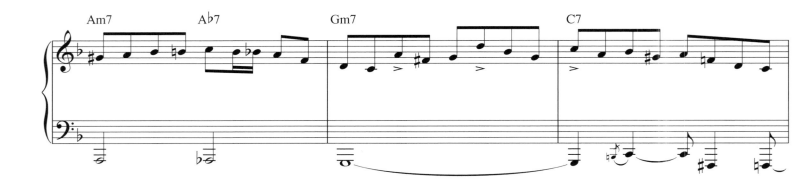

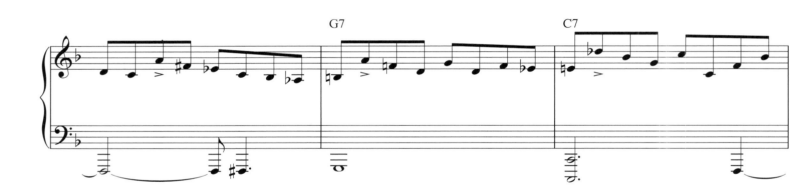

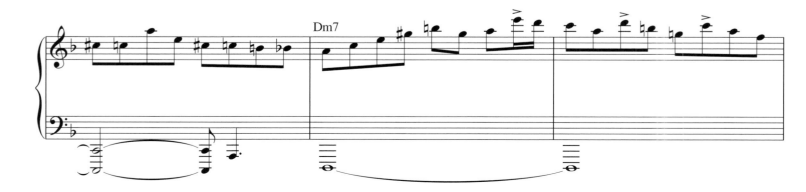

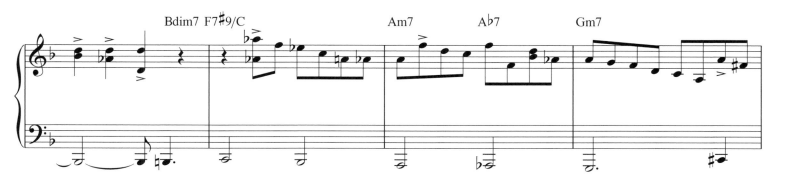

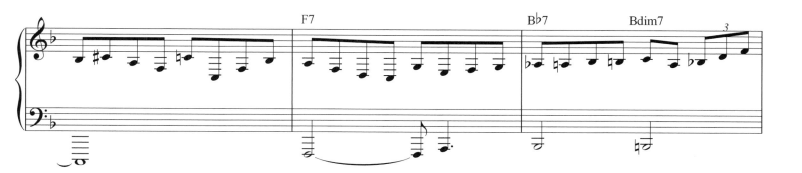

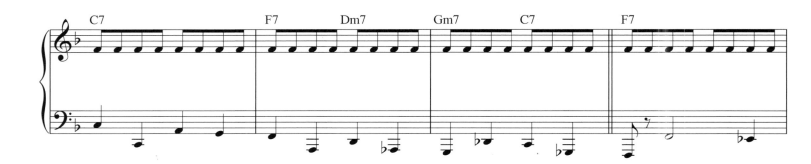

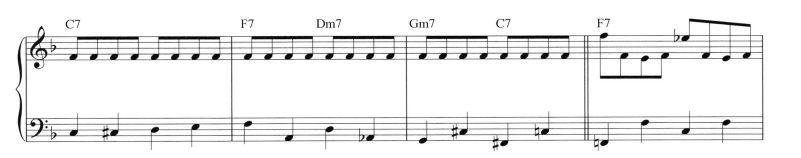

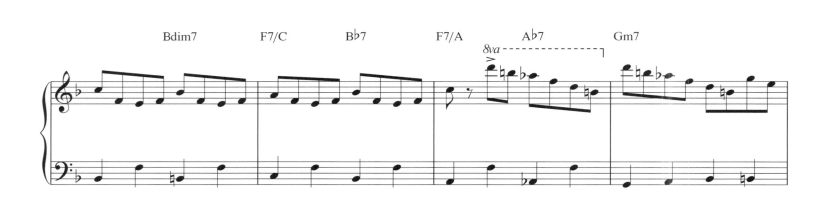

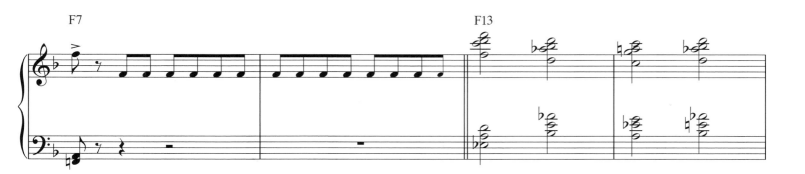

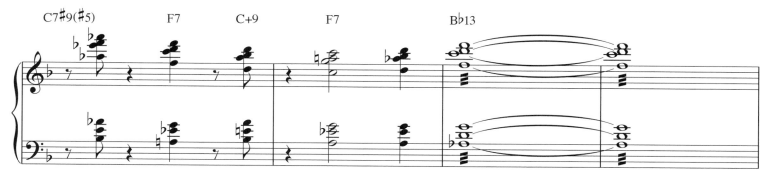

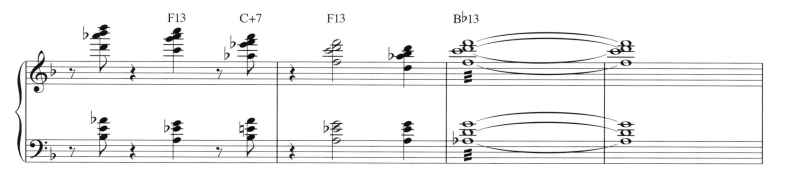

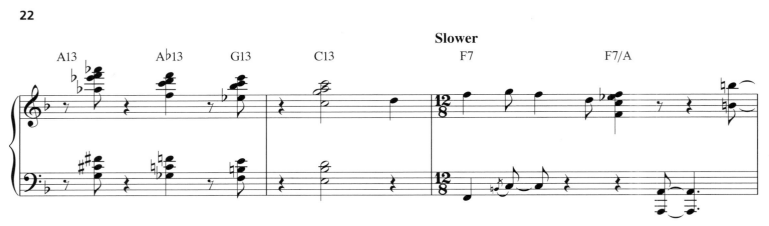

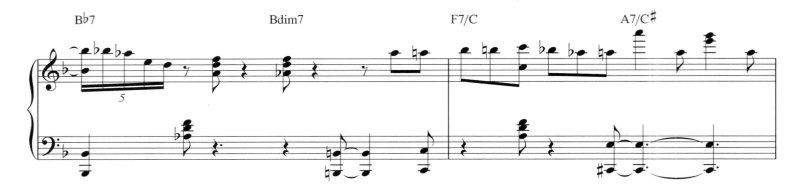

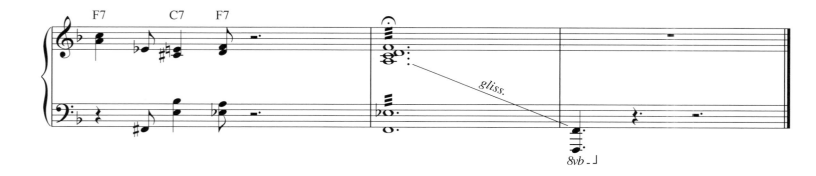

(They Long to Be)
Close to You

Lyric by Hal David
Music by Burt Bacharach

Moderate Rock (♩ = 126)

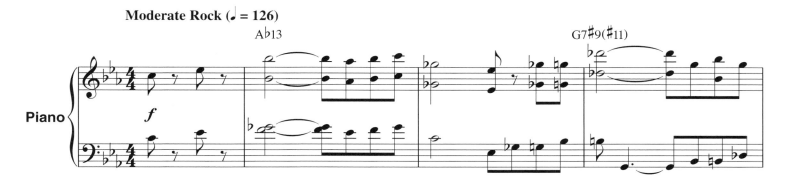

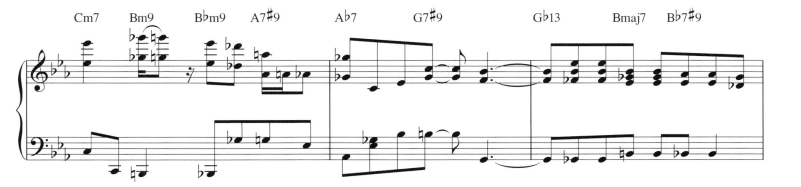

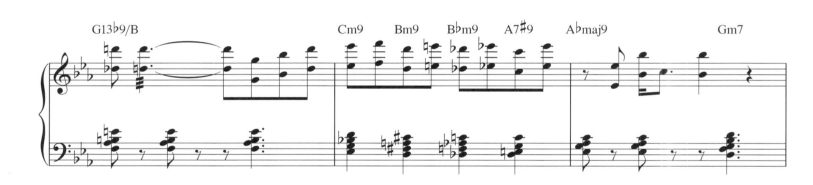

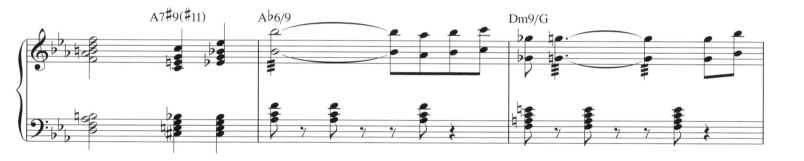

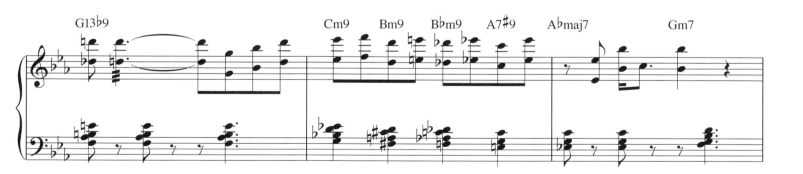

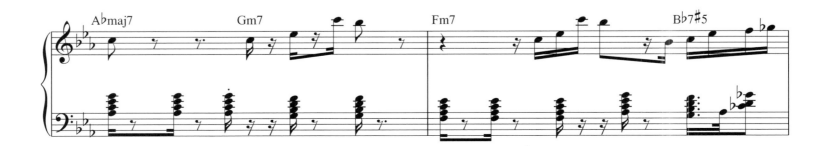

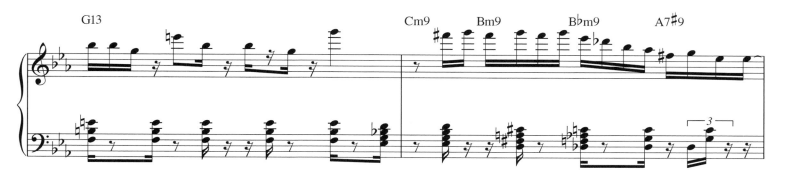

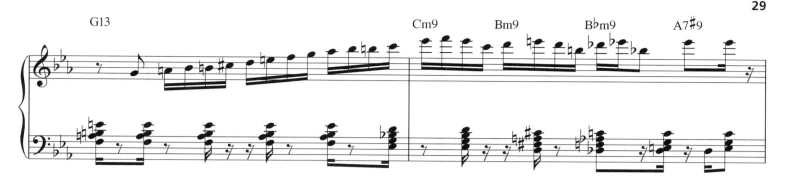

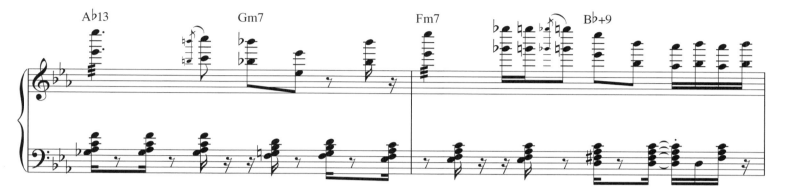

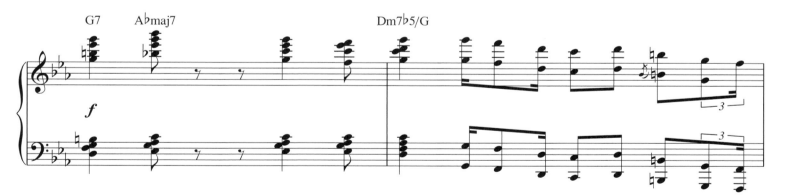

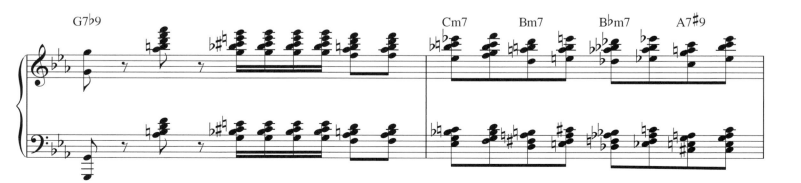

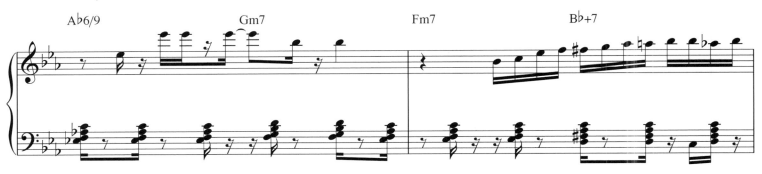

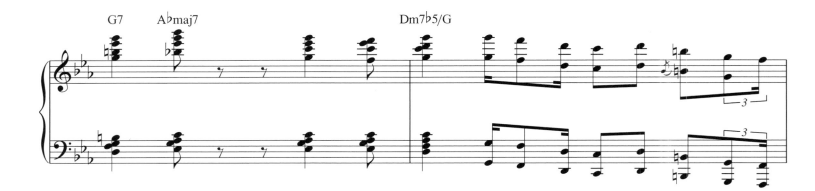

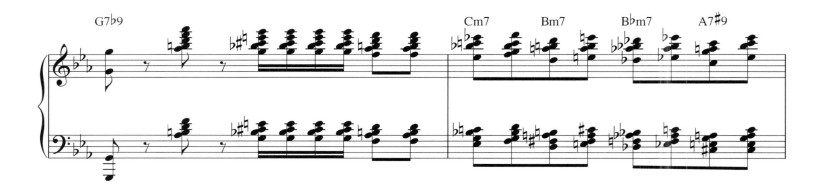

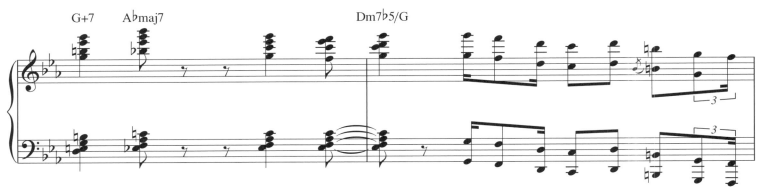

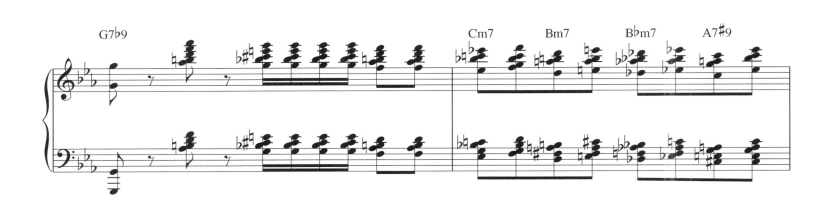

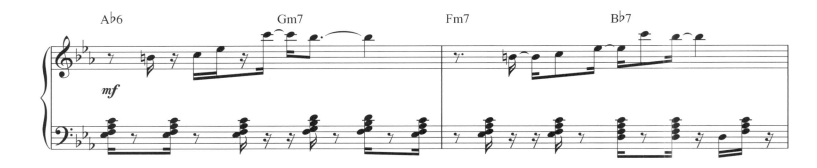

Freeway

By Vince Guaraldi

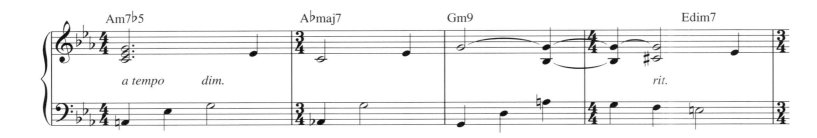

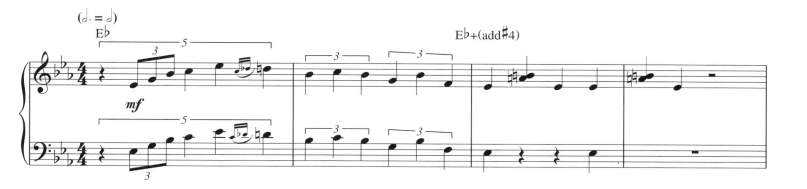

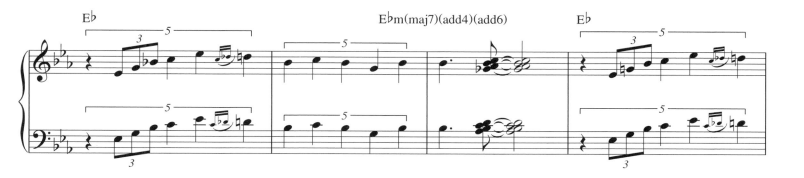

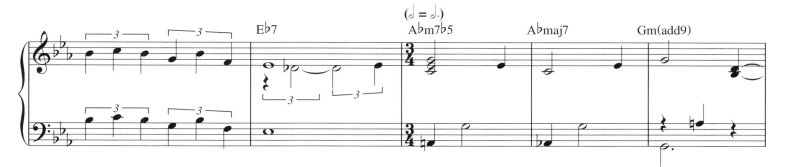

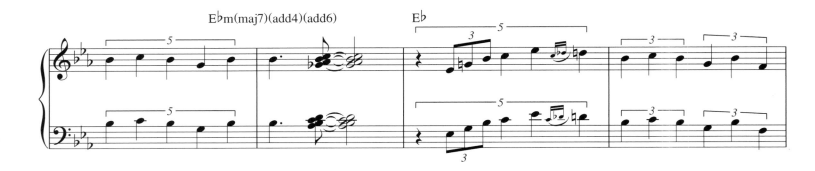

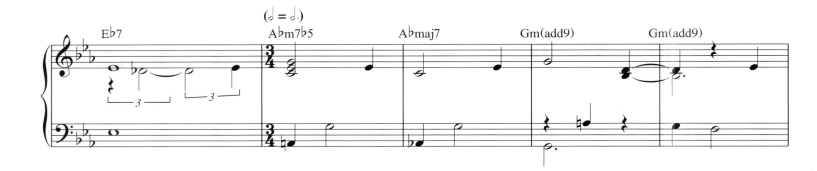

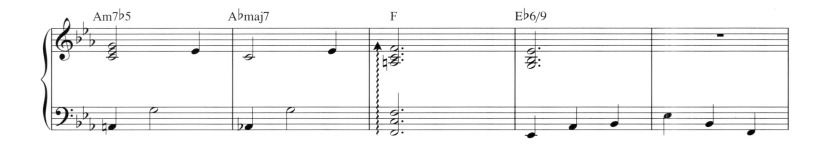

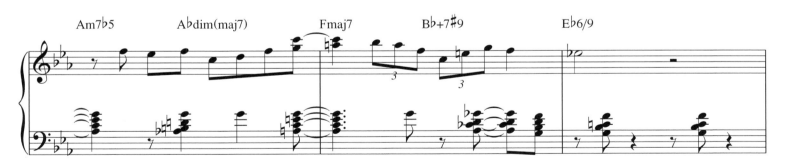

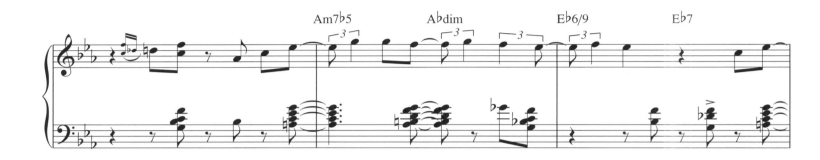

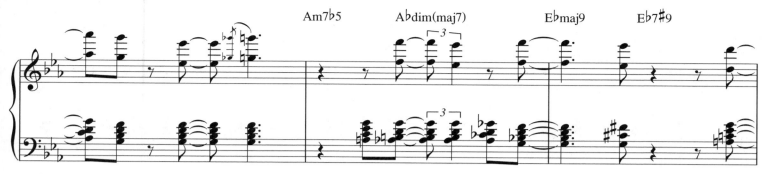

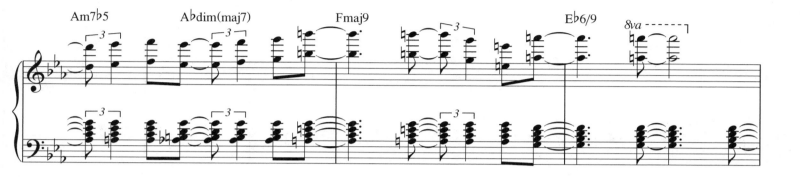

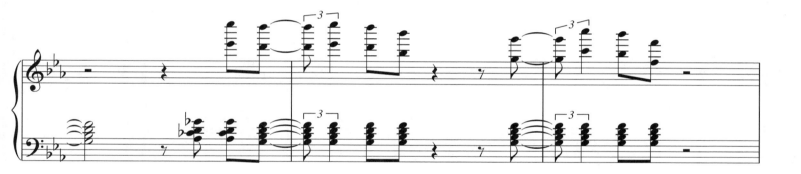

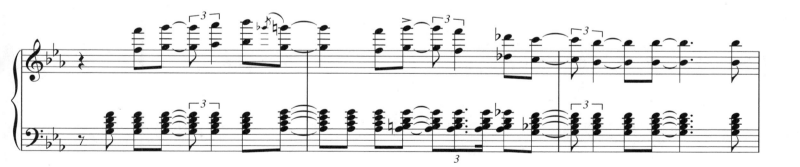

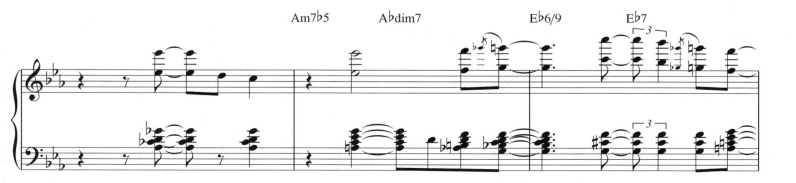

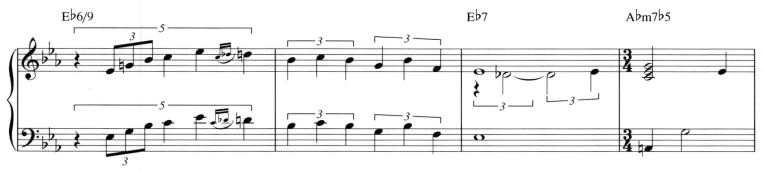

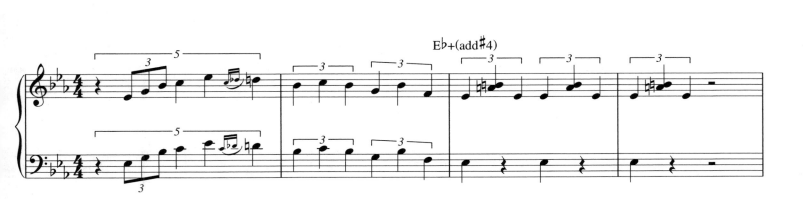

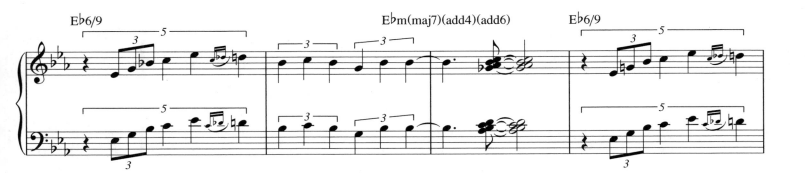

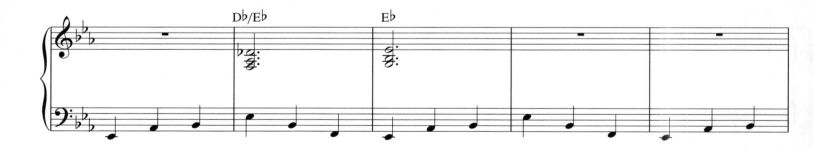

Lonely Woman

Words and Music by Horace Silver

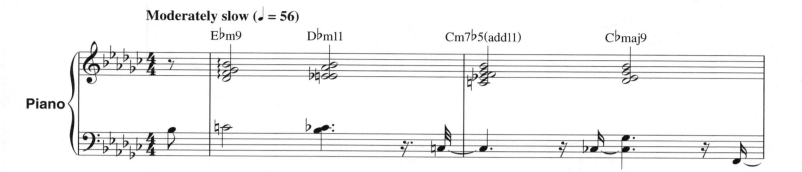

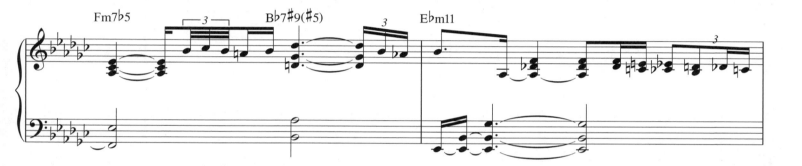

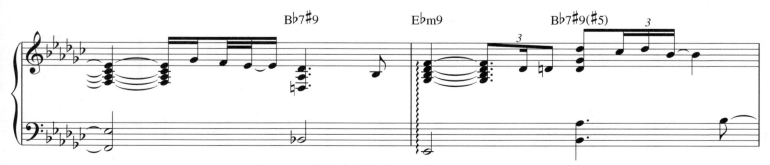

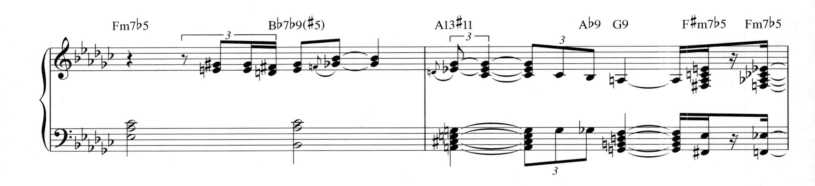

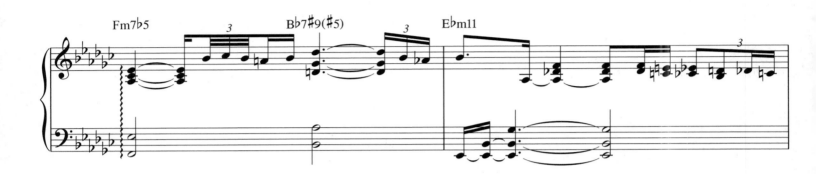

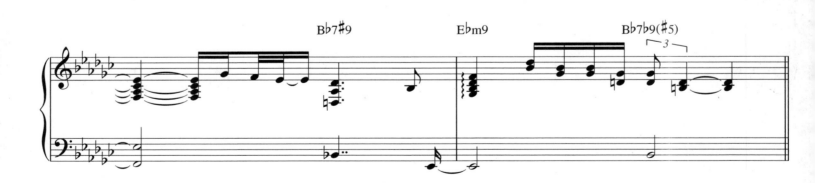

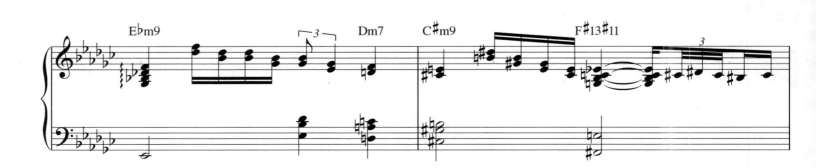

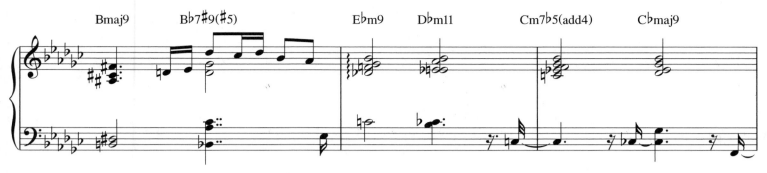

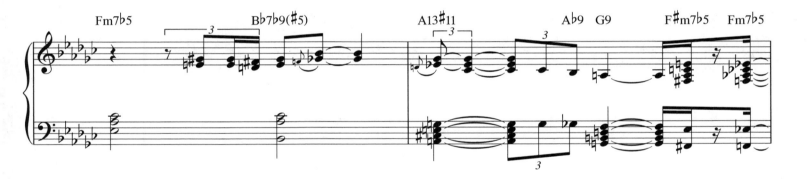

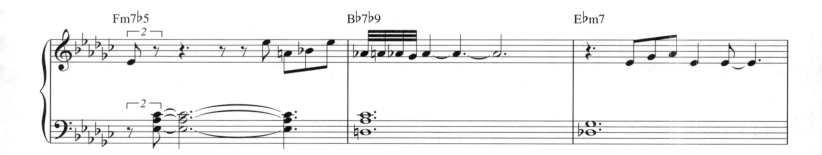

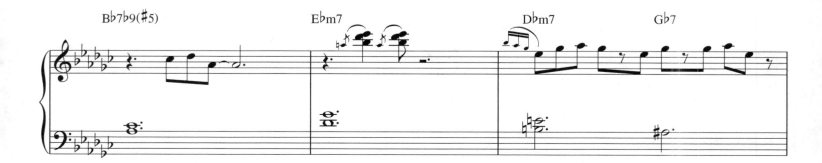

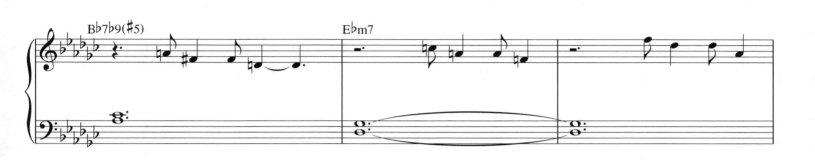

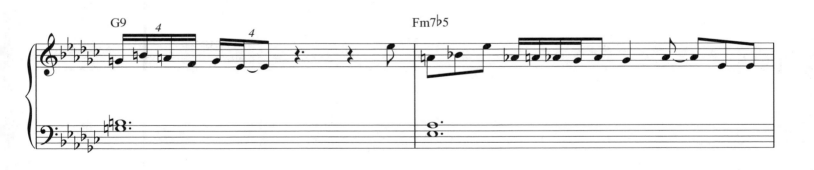

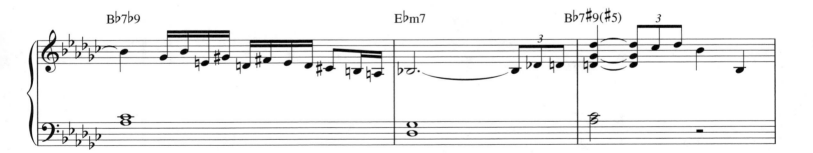

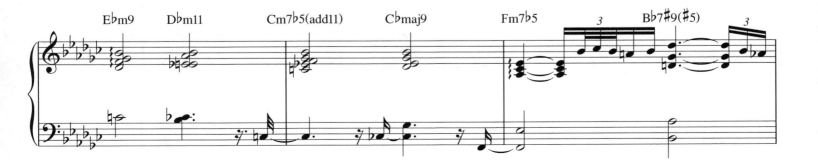

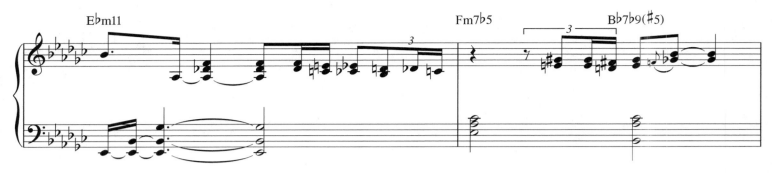

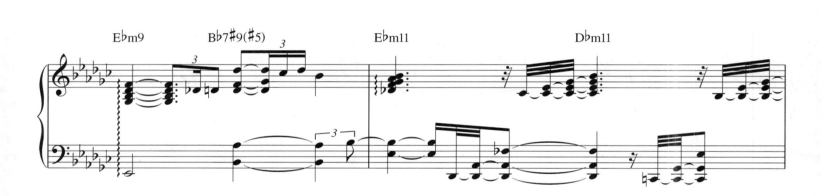

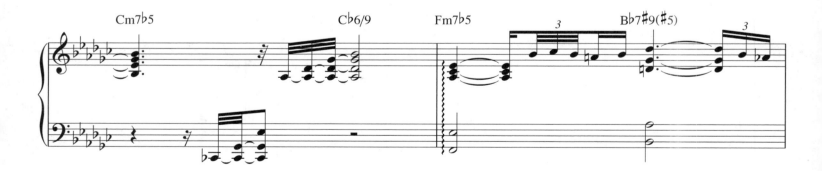

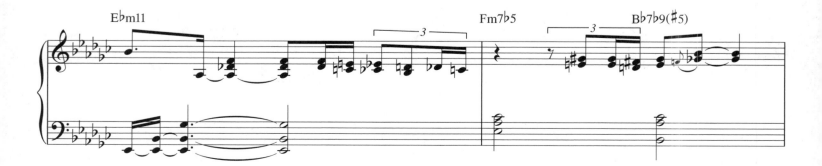

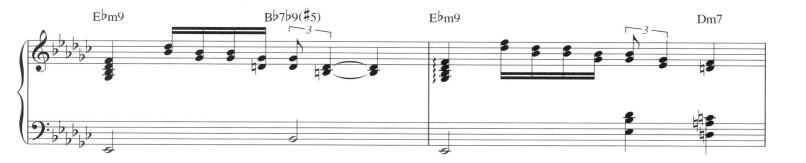

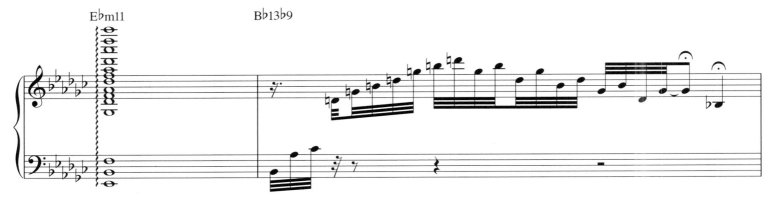

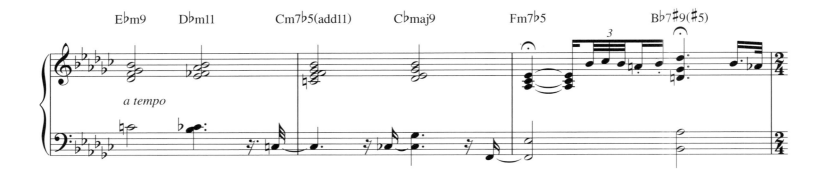

My Foolish Heart
from MY FOOLISH HEART
Words by Ned Washington
Music by Victor Young

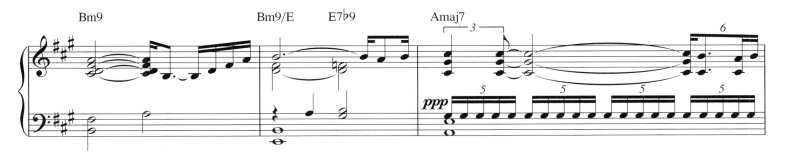

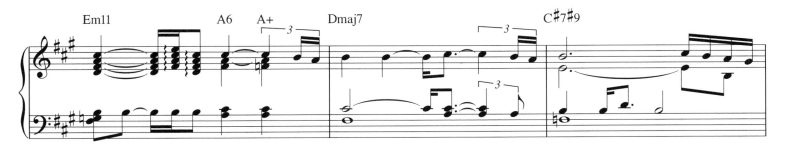

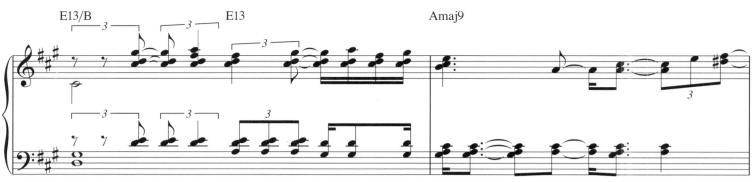

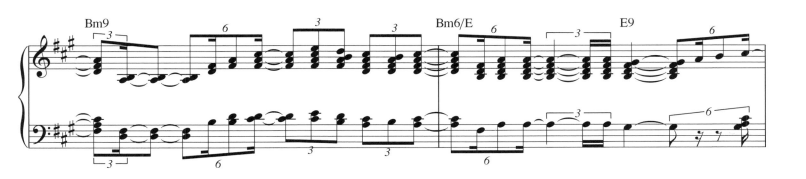

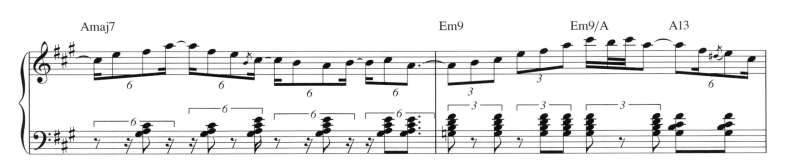

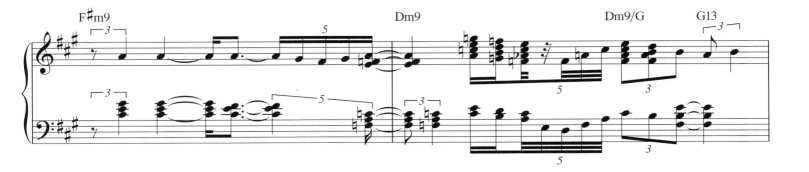

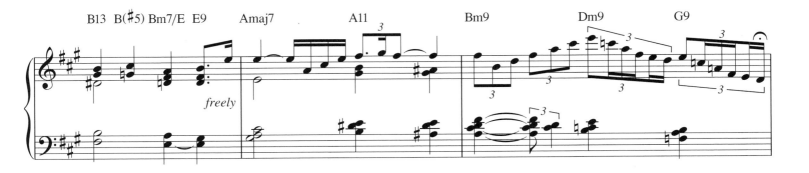
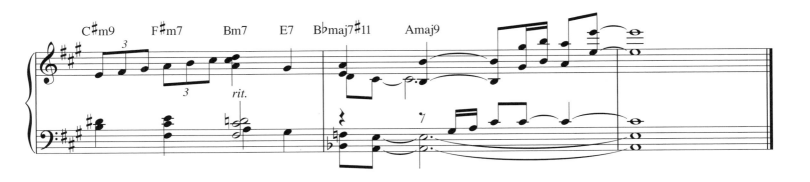

Tin Tin Deo

By Walter Gil Fuller and Luciano Pozo Gonzales

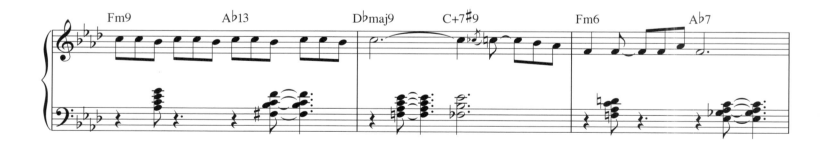

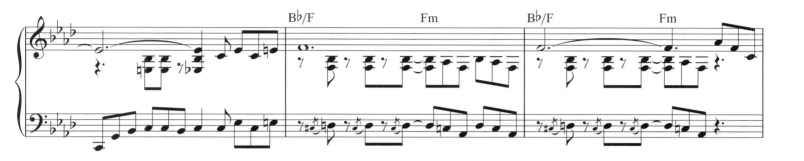

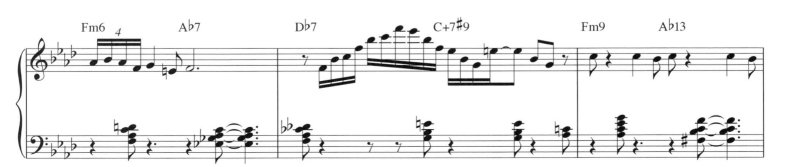

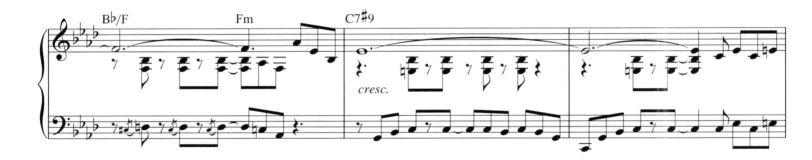

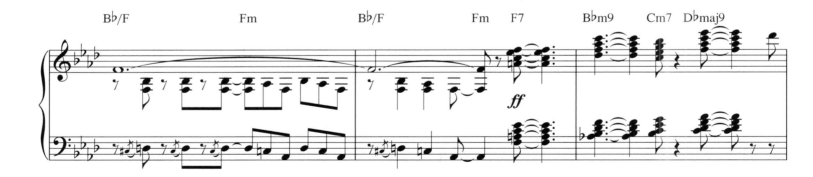

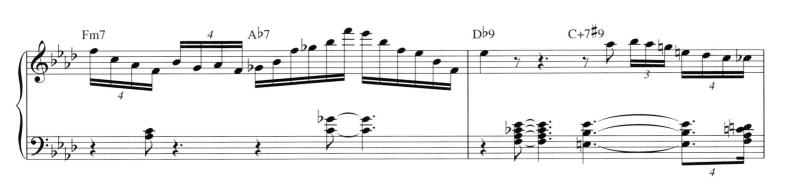

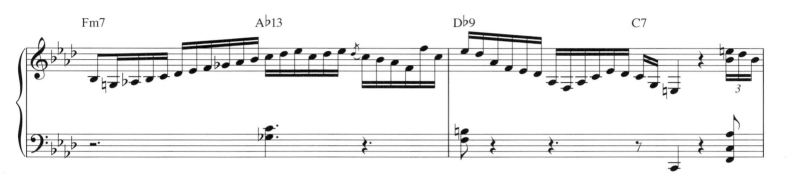

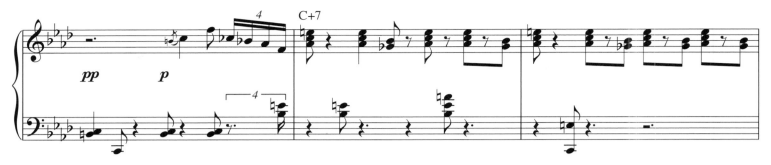

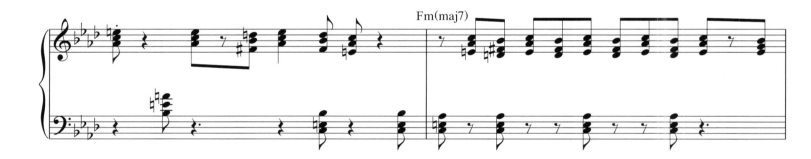

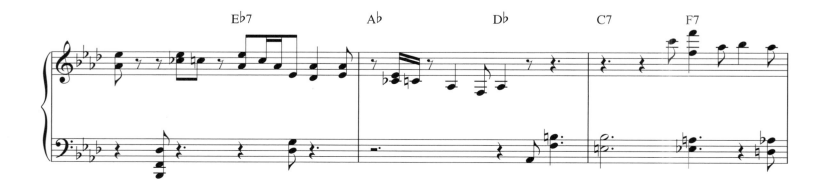

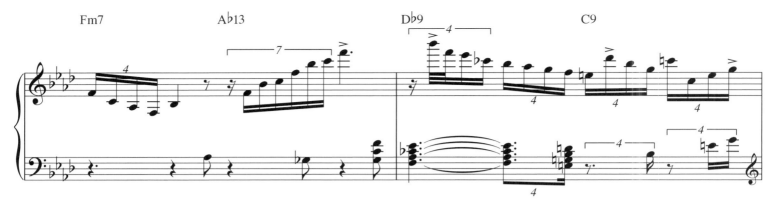

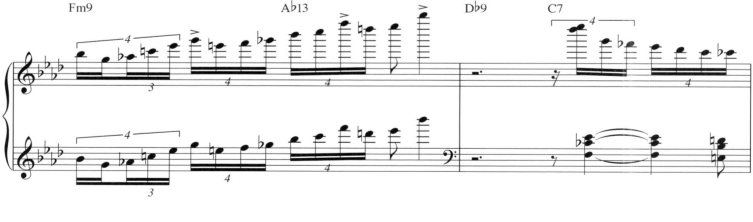

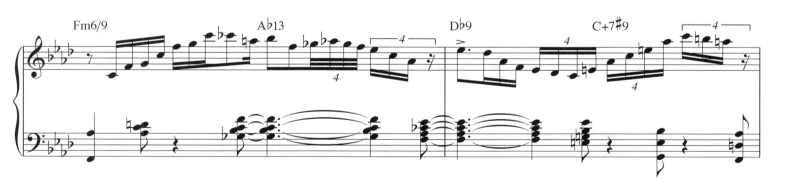

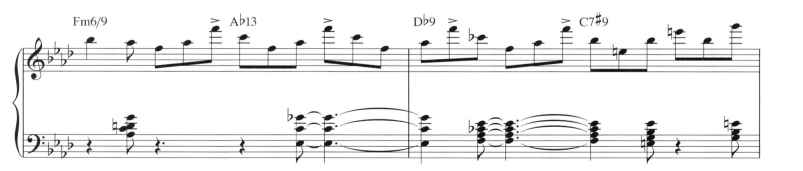

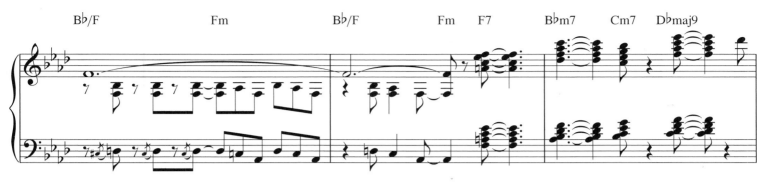

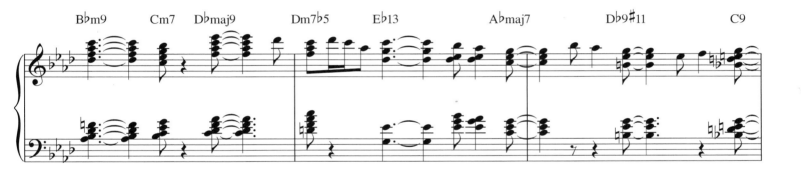

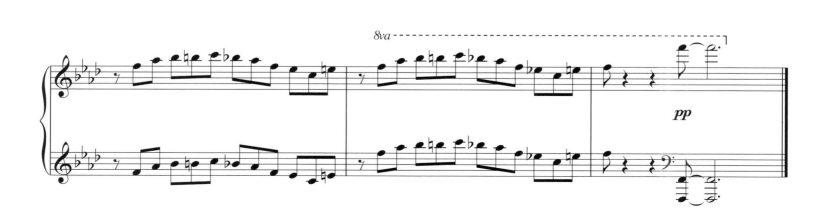

Watch What Happens

from THE UMBRELLAS OF CHERBOURG

Music by Michel Legrand
Original French Text by Jacques Demy
English Lyrics by Norman Gimbel

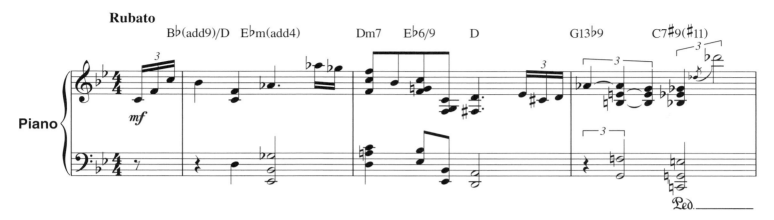

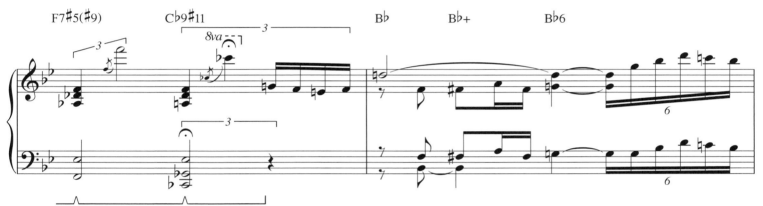

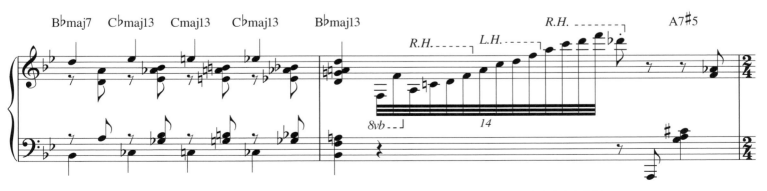

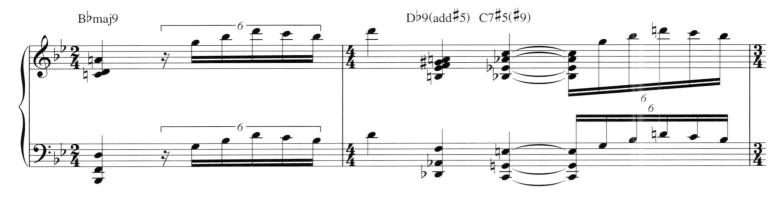

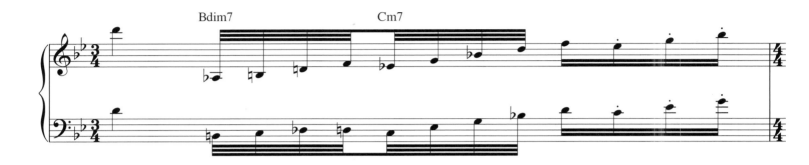

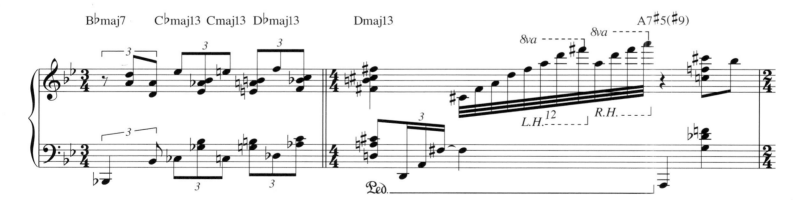

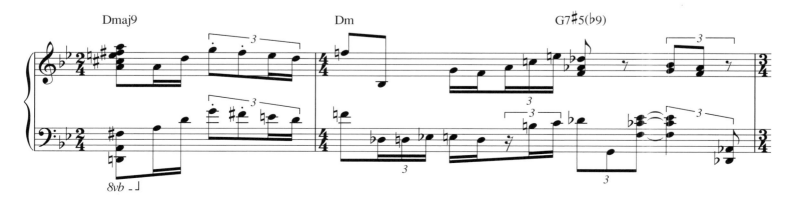

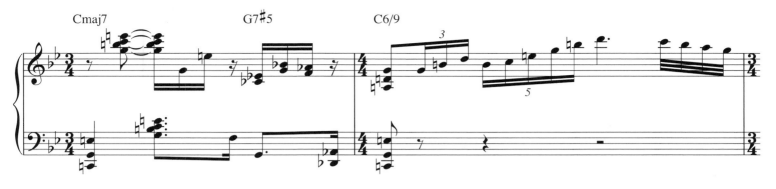

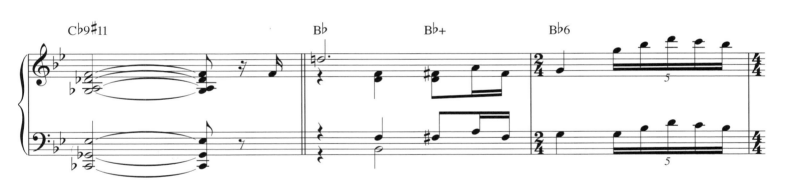

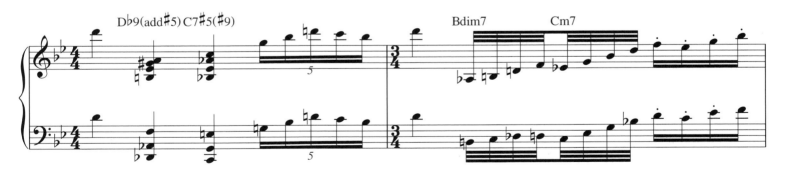

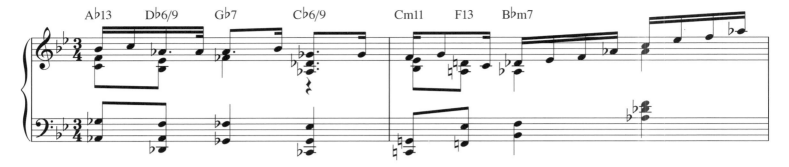

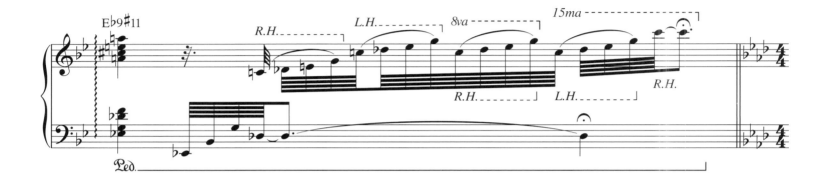

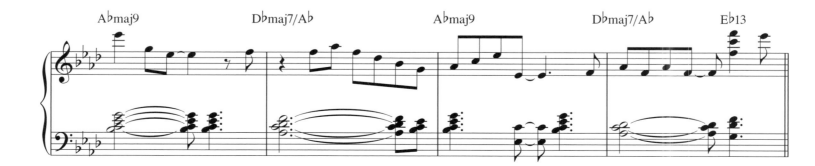

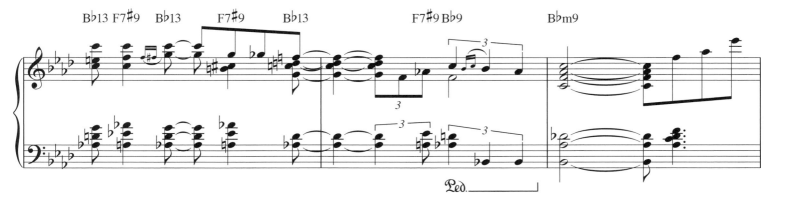

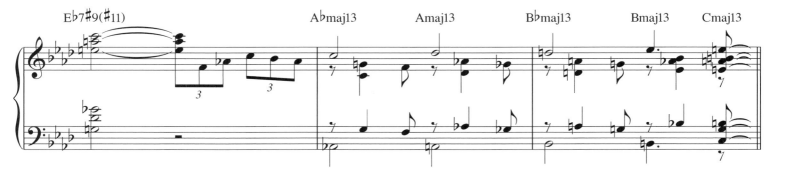

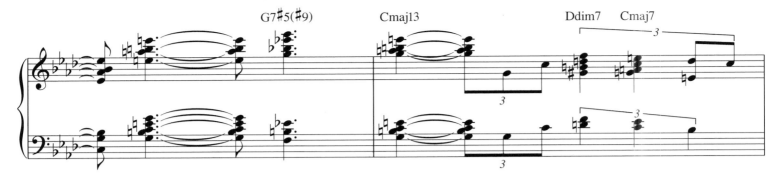

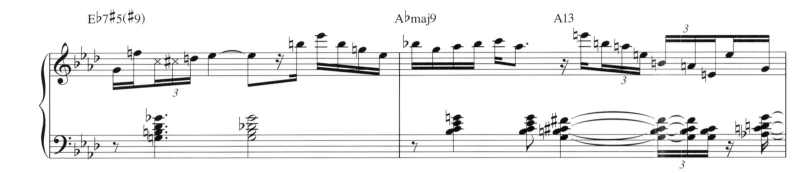

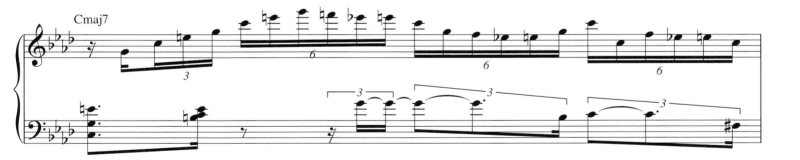

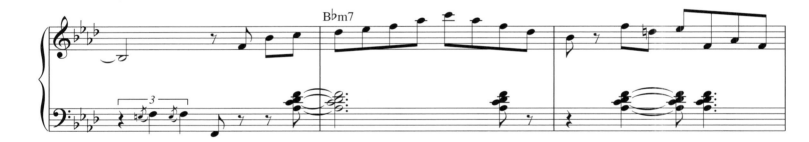

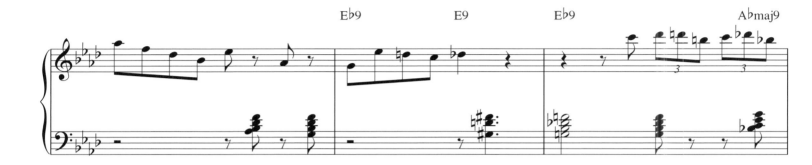

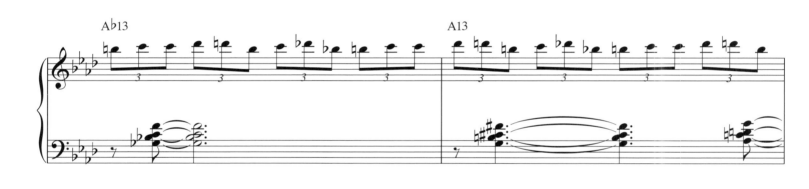

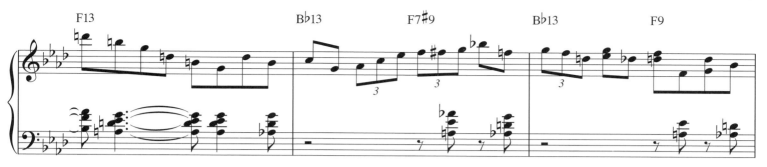

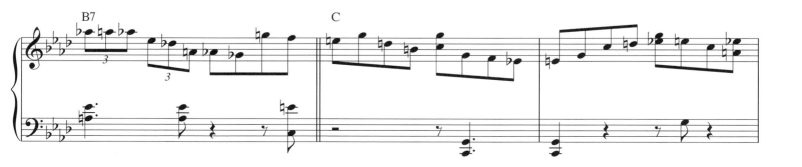

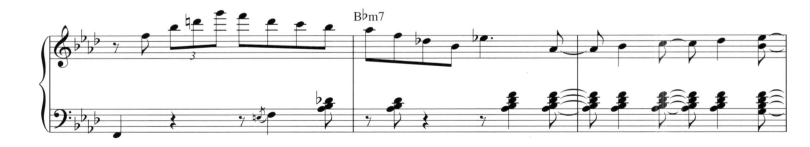

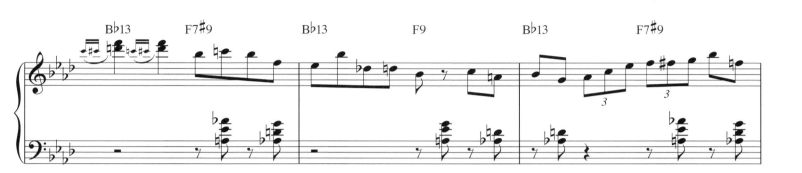

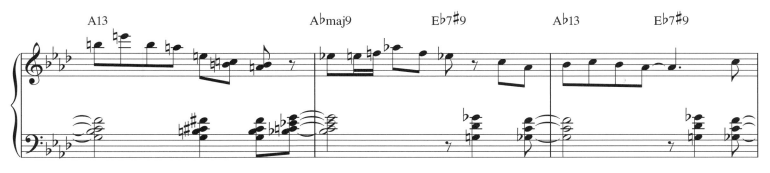

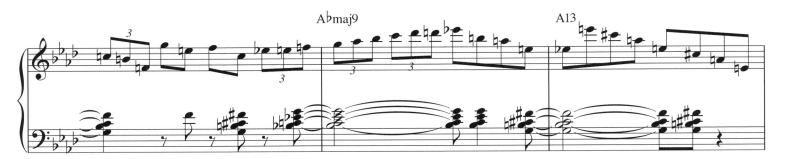

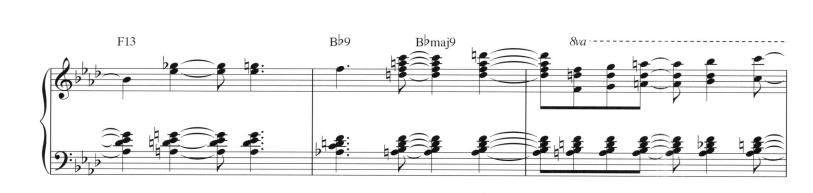

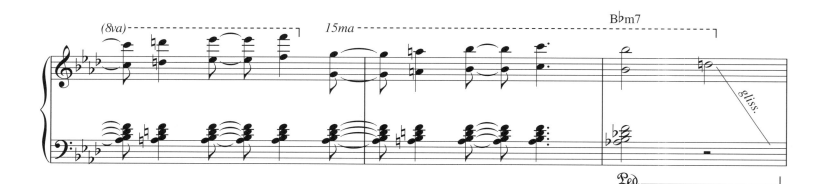

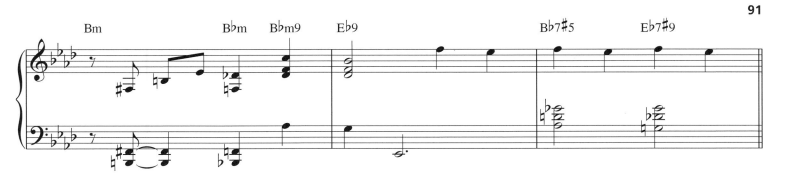

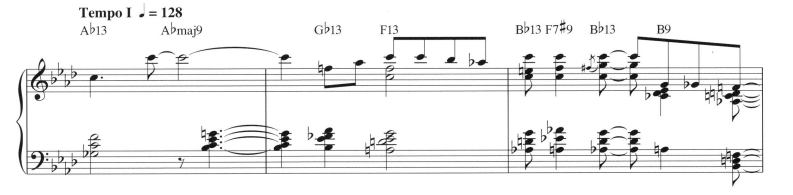

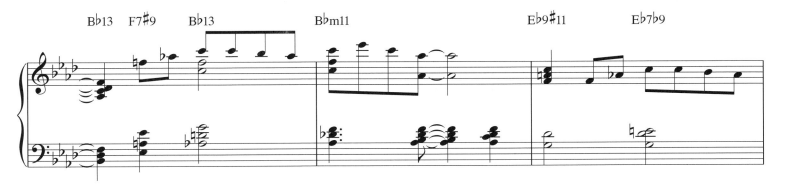

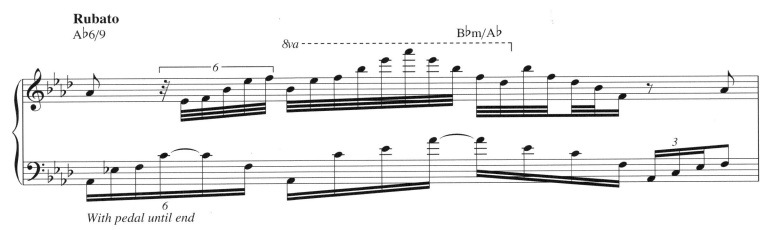

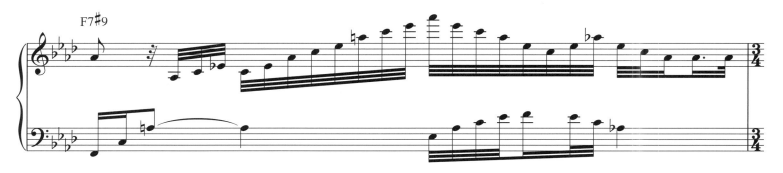

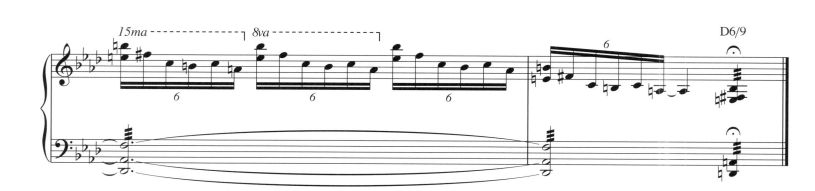